HANDBOOKS OF EUROPEAN NATIONAL DANCES

EDITED BY

VIOLET ALFORD

DANCES OF SWITZERLAND

Plate 1
Lüderen Polka. Emmental

DANCES OF SWITZERLAND

LOUISE WITZIG

PUBLISHED

UNDER THE AUSPICES OF

THE ROYAL ACADEMY OF DANCING

AND THE

LING PHYSICAL EDUCATION ASSOCIATION

LONDON

MAX PARRISH & COMPANY

FIRST PUBLISHED IN 1949 BY
MAX PARRISH & CO LIMITED
55 QUEEN ANNE STREET LONDON W.1
REPRINTED 1953

ILLUSTRATED BY
LUCILE ARMSTRONG
ASSISTANT EDITOR
YVONNE MOYSE

PRINTED IN GREAT BRITAIN
BY JARROLD AND SONS LTD NORWICH
MUSIC PHOTO-SET BY
WOLFGANG PHILIPP ZURICH-HINTEREGG

CONTENTS

Illustrations in Colour, pages 2, 19, 30, 31
Map of Switzerland, page 6

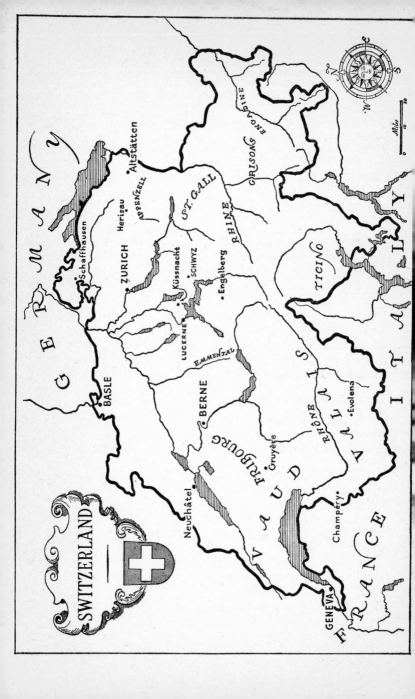

INTRODUCTION

Iɴ considering Swiss tradi-
tions, the geographical situation of the country and the
ethnological constitution of its people must be taken into
account. Small though it is, Switzerland is inhabited by
four different races. On the lakes of Geneva and Neuchâtel
is a French-speaking population; in the East and North
are Alemannic Swiss, speaking German dialects; in the
Grisons Rhaeto-Romanic people speak Romansh, and on
the south side of the Alps are the Ticinese who speak
Italian. Switzerland is indeed a meeting-place of peoples
and cultures, as the following examples of dances will
show.

In Geneva, although close to the south-east gateway into
France, a Polka Bavière is known; in Schaffhausen at the
opposite side of our country a figure of the Française is
danced. In the Rhaeto-Romanic Engadine the Allemanda
has been handed down, and in that same valley two manu-
scripts of the eighteenth and nineteenth centuries were
found containing collections of French Contredanses and
Quadrilles. Thus every part of the country acquires something from another part. All over Switzerland however
the Pair dance was the prevalent form, and the mastery of
about six basic steps and combinations with several
different holds was generally sufficient for dancers to
manage all our traditional dances.

Such a combination of basic forms with varying steps results in delightful figures. Some of the well-known Pair dances have in this way branched out into a number of regional dances, each with its own tune. One of the best-known of these is the Kreuz-Polka (Cross Polka), a favourite in German-speaking Switzerland; its French counterpart, the Polka Piquée, is just as well known. The Schottische has been adapted in various ways; old-fashioned ballroom dances, themselves now partly 'folk', have produced a type of Pair dance common to North-West Europe, and nearly everywhere this is accompanied by sung tunes with verses. In Central Switzerland, where the song is lacking, this type is called Mansechter, in the Emmental Langmuus, a word which connects it in a corrupt form with Langaus, that is the finale of a dance feast.

⁂ THE LÄNDLER TYPE ⁂

The Ländler, out of which perhaps the immortal Waltz grew, is particularly dear to our people. This is the most sprightly of all our dances, and has a specially rich development in the Alps, where it has assumed the character of a Courting dance. It is in the Austrian Alps that it has attained its apogee;* here in Switzerland it begins, somewhat tentatively when first met, developing as we go eastwards. We find it in the German-speaking districts of Central and Eastern Switzerland (Cantons Schwyz and Appenzell) as well as all over the Austrian Alps and in Bavaria. The chief part falls to the man. While the woman spins round by herself, the man stamps his feet on the ground, claps his thighs and snaps his fingers like castanets. He chases the woman in front of him or leaps round her; stamping out the rhythm, he works up the dance, and finally, grasping his girl round the waist, swings her round in a vigorous Pair dance. It is an extremely lively, not to

* See *Dances of Austria* in this series.

say violent, dance, full of excitement, working up to a climax which demands a great deal of skill and endurance on the part of the man. That is the very reason it is dying out. Modern dancing is so much less exacting.

In Central Switzerland the Ländler is known as the Gäuerler, in Appenzell as the Hierig, both meaning the local dance. In Bavaria and Austria it becomes the famous Schuhplattler. The Hierig has developed more figures than the Gäuerler, while the Schuhplattler reaches the full development.

The Clog dance or Bödele—the name comes from the Holzböden, the home-made wooden clogs of the Alpine cowherds—occurs not only in these Courting dances, but the cowherd makes use of it at his pleasure in the course of any dance. He enjoys emphasising the rhythm by the sound of his clogs, and thus gives expression to his delight in his own movements.

꽃 SQUARE DANCES AND LONGWAYS 꽃

Squares are found in French Switzerland and seem to be descendants of the once fashionable Quadrille. They are named Monferrine in Cantons Vaud and Valais; in the Italian-speaking Ticino the Monferrina is well known. They are performed by two or four couples as in a ball-room Quadrille. The main motif is the constant changing of places by each couple, while some of them work up to the changing of partners, and then the excitement grows. The Dutch Vleegerd shows what sort of excitement there can be in this change of partners, the women shrieking as they are tossed across the set to the opposite man who catches his new partner with zest. But most of these types show traces of their formal ballroom origin.

Longways country dances are rare in our country. We know only two, La Matelotte at Champéry, Valais, and the Munoth-Tour at Schaffhausen in the extreme North.

Country folk enjoy miming. Little scenes of love and banter are woven into the dance; for instance the Vögeli Schottische consists of stamping, hand-clapping, shaking of the finger, then a turn followed by the ordinary Schottische round the room. A more complicated example is the Drei Lederni Strömpf from Appenzell. Here each round is preceded by mime: first teasing and caresses, leading to a lover's quarrel, then a reconciliation, forgiveness and a kiss to wind up, each little scene interrupted by a dance interlude. The people of Appenzell love acting, and sometimes local events are mimed between rounds of a Waltz or Polka.

We must mention the Picoulet, well-known in French Switzerland and loved by the children, although danced often enough by students and grown-ups at social gatherings. It is accompanied by singing; the dancers hold hands and skip round in a circle; the leader goes into the middle and proceeds to make all sorts of gestures which must be imitated exactly by the chorus: first with the finger, then with the hand; then come the fist, the elbow, the foot, the head, a new gesture added at every repeat, a Skip Round intervening each time. It is now an amusing game, but may have its origins in something deeper, as may be seen by its parallels in other countries, for example the curious agglomerative ritual of the Seven Jumps, solemnly done by men in Germany, in Holland and as far away as the Basque country.

THE ANCIENT CHAIN DANCE

The Picoulet forms a transition between the Closed Rounds and the Open Rounds or Chain dances, both of which are traditional in the French part of Switzerland, especially in the Gruyère, the Alpine district above Fribourg. There several Chain dances have survived under the name of Coraule, springing from the medieval Carole. This popular name is exceedingly interesting, making a direct connection with the Choros, the great circular dance of Greece.* For the Choros is a living link with the Chorea, the circling of the Chorus in the classical drama.

Some seventy years ago, the story goes, the old stage-coach to Bulle, the most important of the little towns in the Gruyère district, drew up at the inn, and was immediately surrounded by a great Coraule which swept out of the town. It had brought a distinguished visitor, and the revolving coils circled round the coach in honour of the nameless notability seated inside. A charming scene to invoke in these days of headlong motor traffic.

The Coraules are accompanied by songs in the interesting dialect of the region, and occasionally the song proper is followed by an instrumental refrain. All Coraules begin as a Round, then with the refrain break up into a Pair dance, frequently a Schottische. Here then is a medieval dance-form in a state of transition into a Pair dance. Of a similar type is the Feulatare, which means La Folâtre, the Mad dance. It comes from Champéry in the Valais, and now-adays two or four couples usually take up their position in the middle of the great circle. While it moves round them, the couples in the middle spin round on themselves with short quick steps, looking like spinning tops. Then the chain breaks into couples and these in their turn take up the spinning, while the middle couples move out into a wider circle and a quieter motion. Thus the figures alternate, the spinning in the middle and the spinning on the outside.

✥ THE ALLEMANDE ✥

This interestingly named dance is found in both German and French Switzerland. It is called Alewander or Alle-mandler in German dialects. In Appenzell it is also known as Schwöbli (derived from Schwaben or Swabia), which seems to point to its country of origin.

* See *Dances of Greece* in this series

Indeed the Allemandes are almost certainly descended from old German promenade dances which became fashionable all over Western Europe, the tunes of which were much used, at least in rhythm though not for dancing, by composers of the seventeenth and eighteenth centuries. We have but to name Beethoven for such compositions in the original 3/4 rhythm, while Bach and Purcell, to mention but two, used a stylised 4/4 Allemande in their Suites. Their main characteristic is a measured walk of the couples round a wide circle followed by a chain, which chain is itself followed by the turning of each couple on the spot. They usually end with a Gallop round the circle.

❧ SOME RITUAL DANCES ❧

The Maypole. Switzerland is a veritable storehouse of ancient rituals carried out to the present day. This short survey cannot possibly do justice to them, but we will begin with a glance at a well-known form of spring rite—the Maypole with its dance. In Canton Basle the young fir is tied to the beam of the well-house; in the Ticino the Maggiolata is a Round sung and danced round a birch tree, but at Champéry, in the Val d'Illiez, Valais, a plaited ribbon dance is executed round the May tree by sixteen dancers, men and women, each holding the end of a ribbon which they plait round the pole.

The Millwheel. In the Alpine valleys of German Switzerland, and the four original cantons of Switzerland, the people have preserved the Mühlerad (Millwheel), or sometimes for the sake of modernity the Mühle Schottische. This is for men only, a sure mark of some ancient ritual. Eight men run round in a circle, four of them then lie flat on their backs pressing their feet together in the centre of the circle. The remaining four take them by the arms, and slowly turn them upon the ground like a wheel turning. The music is a march or a Schottische played on accordion or clarinet. An imposing sight in its quiet way. It seems likely that, in Switzerland, it was once a solar symbol, for apart from agriculture the sun plays an immensely important part in the pastoral life of our Alps. The sun wheel is a favourite motif in our folk art, and is frequently seen carved and painted upon chalets and utensils of Alpine herdsmen and farmers. It may well have found symbolic representation in the dance of the cowmen.

Leafy Fools and Kläuse. We have masked dances of great anthropological value. At Carnival time, in Schwyz, the Nüssler dance is still performed. The Nüssler, as the men themselves are called, are dressed in *Blätzlichleid*—Leafy Clothes—and wear masks on their faces, carry a strap of bells over their shoulders and a magical twig broom in their hands. They assemble in Rotts, troops accompanied by drummers, and dance from inn to inn all day long till dark. The drummers beat a strange and intoxicating rhythm, almost impossible to seize; the dance is as strange, made up of brief leaping movements. Each Nüssler dances by himself without relation to his fellows, yet the whole Rott moves about as a whole, their shoulder bells jingling without cessation. Similar processions are known in Canton Appenzell, where maskers go about on New Year's Eve, St. Sylvester's Day—hence their name of Sylvester-Kläuse. Their fantastic costumes with richly decorated head-dresses are radically different from the Schwyz costumes; the essential features are the enormous bells and the leaping movements, always a primitive form of male ritual dancing. Both Nüssler and Kläuse are probably connected with the driving-out of Winter and evil spirits.

Belled Fools. We must look at the Shrovetide dance of the Röllelibutzen at Altstätten in the Rhine valley (Canton St. Gall). Somewhat like the famous Austrian Perchten, they wear an elaborate and beautiful head-dress and masks, while a strap of leather holding the bells—the *Rölleli*—is slung over one shoulder. They carry small squirts, which they fill with water at the fountain to sprinkle people, especially the unmarried girls. They solemnly march in a great Polonaise, under the orders of their Butzenköni (King of the Maskers) and his officers, all mounted on horseback, surrounded by throngs of spectators.

THE NATIONAL FEDERATION OF SWISS COSTUME

Influences from North and South, from eastern and western cultures have met and blended in our country. In the course of centuries they have produced a many-sided national inheritance of which we are naturally proud. The Swiss Trachtenvereinigung, Fédération Nationale des Costumes et Coutumes Suisses, has undertaken the cultivation and preservation of this heritage. Dances, songs, costumes, folk art and the customs of the people, all these traditions are a racial treasure, which though threatened by the impact of this modern industrial era yet preserve their significance, and are still a source of joy in our national life.

﹛ MUSIC ﹜

Country Instruments. Our country has produced a rich and beautiful harvest of indigenous dance-music. Innumerable hand-written scores and music books have fortunately been preserved, and many of the airs contained therein are still in use amongst the people in the memories of peasant musicians who, unable to read written music, follow the tradition of their forefathers.

The combination of instruments in the old peasant bands was very different before the introduction of that pervading instrument, the accordion. In Appenzell the original band consisted of strings, fiddles, 'cellos, double-bass with a dulcimer. This old instrument is becoming rare to-day. The old Sepplimusik of the Grisons consisted of strings only. In the Valais (south-west), which is very conservative, we still find drums and fifes, a particularly striking kind of old music. In western Switzerland wind instruments predominate, but the accordion is seldom absent. Indeed it is so popular to-day that it has worked its way into nearly every peasant band.

Dance-Songs. Sung dances are not so frequent as in many countries owing, one supposes, to the liking for village bands. There are however verses for the Moléson Coraule in the real medieval style, but as a rule the dancers only sing when they reach the refrain

A Moléson, à Moléson!

The Moléson is the dominating mountain of the region, and the home of the famous Ranz des Vaches, sung as the herds come down from their high summer pastures. The verses of the Coraules, like those of the Ranz des Vaches, are in the dialect of the Gruyère, akin to the Provençal of the far-away South, indeed the Canton of Fribourg marks the northernmost bastion of that ancient tongue.

Away to the North, the Appenzell Polka warns the sleeping Babeli—

Babeli dreams, Babeli dreams,
Don't fall out of bed!

while the favourite Lauterbach, a Courting dance, variants of which are known from Alsace to Austria, says, with probably an erotic meaning, to the tune known as 'The Dutchman's little wee dog',

I lost my stocking at Lauterbach
And I can't go without it.

Jodelling. Although jodels are no part of dancing, this form of musical cry is so connected with the Alps and the Alpine folk that to entirely ignore it would be a disappointment to readers. A mountain cry in high falsetto is known right across Central Europe, and by way of the uplands of the French Massif Central links with those of the Pyrenees, those of the Pyrenees with those of the Spanish Cantabrian mountains, which themselves continue westwards to peter out in the *Riflido* of the Galician coastal heights. The cries of the Pyrenees are merely cries, not used with folk song except sometimes amongst the Spanish Basques. That of the French Basques, the *Irrintzina*, is terrible in its wailing, shrieking rise and fall—an antique death-cry by all accounts. It is in the Alps that it becomes a real musical expression as well as a simple cow-call. The last is 'natural' jodelling, the first can be reduced to bars and intervals. Thousands of Swiss folk songs have a jodel refrain in which the singer's voice shoots up from a good, rich bass to an A in alt. There are famous jodelling clubs and choirs, for whom jodel music has been written in parts. In these a trained man's voice will soar over the others as pure as a chorister's treble, while the lower parts may be jodels too on lower notes. The Austrian Alps show another style, more suave, often heart-rending, and in both Swiss and Austrian Alps women jodel as readily as men.

This very characteristic Alpine use of the voice begins tentatively, but already in two or three parts, in the tragically famous Vercors region to the east of Grenoble between the Isère and the Drac. It probably reaches its highest musical development in Austria. Although, as already said, jodels are no part of dancing, yet at the climax of a Gäuerler there may be a sudden outburst from an excited young man as he leaps round and before his spinning partner, and at the break-up of a dance, coming away from the valley inn, the cries ring through the night soaring and falling as though they were borne on wings.

⁂ COSTUME ⁂

As in all countries which have preserved costume those of Switzerland are regional, not national. So local are they that they cannot even be called cantonal, almost every valley possessing its own. In the large Canton of Berne, the Oberland, Simmental, Emmental, Haslital and the Guggisberg have each their own costume, differing in many ways from what tourists think is the costume of Berne. The valleys of the long Canton of Valais each possess their own costume, so that one can say at once this girl is from the Lötschental, that woman from Evolena. The National Federation of Swiss Costume has done an immense work here, differentiating the costumes, and bringing to life once more the local dressmakers, weavers, knitters, silver-filigree workers.

So lovely, intricate and varied are the Swiss costumes that mention can be made only of outstanding ones, beginning with the shimmering gold lace halo caps on the heads of the women of St. Gall. Women of Appenzell and Schwyz show lovely spreading lace wings on their heads, while the Appenzell cowmen's best costume is gorgeous with its heavily worked straps and braces, whereon cows move in silver procession across the wearer's stalwart chest, with a single earring in the shape of a silver spoon dropping from his right ear, and a wreath of Alpine flowers round his black felt hat. One of the most striking of the revived costumes is that of the High Engadine, a medieval gown of sumptuous scarlet, with its wide white collar to set off the brilliant colour, and a plastron embroidered with flowers of the most exquisite Renaissance design.

PLATE 1. Emmental costume is a good type of that of Canton Berne, though not the costume seen in Berne itself. The corslet bodice is yellow in front instead of black; the silver chains hanging from bosses at each corner of the yoke are a sign of wealth, and can be merely double or sixfold. The flat *Schwefelhut* is yellow and stiffened with sulphur, but a black cap of horsehair lace with outstanding wings may be worn instead.

PLATE 2. Canton Unterwalden is divided into Obwalden and Nidwalden by the great forest. Engelberg is in Obwalden, but that district has been so strongly influenced by Nidwalden that the latter's costume is worn. It is very ornate for the women, with lovely silver ornaments and silver spoonlike comb in the side of the hair. The man's blouse shows most beautiful light embroidery.

PLATE 3. Costume of Evolena, Canton Valais. The chief characteristic is the flat straw hat trimmed with ribbon bows. A quiet and warm costume for both men and women. Married women wear a white cap under the flat hat.

PLATE 4. The Gruyère dress is of hand-woven linen or wool, in summer wide sleeves to the elbow, on feast days three-quarter or long sleeves of the same as the dress. A very large bib marks the apron, while on the shoulders is a three-cornered kerchief with white chainstitch or pearl-bead embroidery. A black lace cap or a wide straw hat with flat black bows and an end to tie under the chin. The cowmen are the celebrated Armaillis, who wear a short blue linen or cotton coat embroidered with white stitching and an edelweiss. Short sleeves with puffs show bare, brown arms, but for best, white shirt sleeves ironed into accordion pleats round the arm, not downwards. The tiny round cap is bound with black velvet.

Plate 2
Alewander
Engelberg, Obwalden

❧ NOTE ❧

Swiss folk are particularly proud of and devoted to their wonderful costumes. Before admission as a member of their National Federation of Costumes and Customs everyone must promise to respect his or her costume, to wear it correctly in all details, and never to use it for 'fancy dress'. Therefore respect them too. If you attempt to reproduce one do so seriously, and refrain from adding anything to suit your own fancy.

The Editor

DATES AND OCCASIONS WHEN DANCING
MAY BE SEEN

December 6th, St. Nicholas' Night — Klausjagen with lighted head-dresses at Küssnacht.

New Year's Eve and January 13th — Sylvester-Kläuse, the same sort of dancers as above, at Herisau and other villages in Appenzell.

January 13th, 20th or 27th — Basle. Vogel Gryff: traditional civic men-animals.

Carnival, the last days before Lent — Dance of the Nüssler at Schwyz and Steinen. The Röllelibutzen at Altstätten, St. Gall, in the Rhine valley.

Chiefly during the summer — Folk dance and costume meetings, often on a mountainside, organised by the Fédération Nationale des Costumes et Coutumes Suisses.

Information can be ascertained from the above Federation (Schweizerische Trachtenvereinigung), Heimethuus, Uraniabrücke, Zurich 1.

THE DANCES

TECHNICAL EDITOR, MURIEL WEBSTER
ASSISTED BY KATHLEEN P. TUCK

ABBREVIATIONS
USED IN DESCRIPTION OF STEPS AND DANCES

r—right ⎱ referring to   R—right ⎱ describing turns or
l—left ⎰ hand, foot etc.   L—left ⎰ ground pattern
C—clockwise   C-C—counter-clockwise

For descriptions of foot positions and explanations of any ballet terms the following books are suggested for reference:

A Primer of Classical Ballet (Cecchetti method). Cyril Beaumont.

First Steps (R.A.D.). Ruth French and Felix Demery.

The Ballet Lover's Pocket Book. Kay Ambrose.

REFERENCE BOOKS FOR DESCRIPTION OF FIGURES:

The Scottish Country Dance Society's Publications. Many volumes, from Thornhill, Cairnmuir Road, Edinburgh 12.

The English Folk Dance and Song Society's Publications Cecil Sharp House, 2 Regent's Park Road, London N.W.1.

The Country Dance Book I–VI. Cecil J. Sharp. Novello & Co., London.

The poise of body is upright and strong, and shows the characteristics of the dances—simplicity and vigour.

The hand grasps are various and form one of the most interesting features of the dances.

1. Waltz grasp. Man places r arm round partner's waist, she placing her l hand on his r shoulder. With his l hand he grasps her r hand at shoulder height, arm nearly straight.

2. Closed grasp. Man places both hands on partner's waist while she places her hands on his shoulders. (In both 1 and 2, partners lean away from one another.)

3. Trüll grasp. Partners face each other with l hands on hips; woman grasps with her r hand the man's r forefinger which he raises at head height and points downward. This grasp, which is very loose, enables the woman to turn on the spot under the joined r arms.

4. Waist grasp. Partners stand side by side, man on L of woman; man places his r arm round partner's waist, grasping her r hand on her r hip, and with his l hand he grasps her l hand in front of their waists in a 'leading' position.

5. Arch grasp. Partners stand side by side with l hands as in waist grasp; the r hands are grasped and raised above the girl's head, forming a frame for her face. This grasp is similar to that explained in Scottish Country Dance books under 'Allemande'.

The technique used in these dances is simple, with very little extension of feet or knees. The placing of the feet is not accurate so that 1st or 3rd positions are not used in the descriptions.

	MUSIC *Beats*
Polka Step. This step starts with a step and finishes with a hop as in a slow or half-time Polka step—	
step, close up, step and hop.	
It may be danced forward, sideways and turning.	
Schottische Step. This step may also be danced forward, sideways and turning. In 2/4 tempo it is similar to the Scottish 'Skip change of step'. In 3/4 tempo, as in 'A Moléson', it is danced as follows—	
A. TURNING	
Step sideways on l foot turning to R.	1
Close r foot to l foot, still turning.	and
Step sideways on l foot, turning to R (half-turn).	2
Raise r leg slightly sideways, inclining body to side of raised foot.	3
Repeat on r foot, still turning to R (to complete the turn).	

Step forward on l foot.	1
Close r foot to l foot.	and
Step forward on l foot.	2
Swing r leg slightly forwards.	3

Rheinländer Step

Step sideways on l foot.	1
Close r foot to l foot.	2
Step forward diagonally on l foot.	3
Hop on l foot, swing r leg across.	4

N.B.—Knee and ankle are not extended when leg is swung across.

The timing of this step in 2/4 tempo would be	1 & 2 &
The timing of this step in 3/4 tempo would be	1 & 2 3

Mazurka Step. This resembles the Swedish but not the Polish Mazurka step.

Step forward on l foot with a stamp.	1
Spring r foot to l foot, swinging l leg forward (coupé dessous).	2
Hop on r foot with l leg raised in front.	3

This step is usually danced three times on l foot and is followed by one Waltz step forward to repeat on the other foot.

VALSE FRAPPÉE

✷✷✷✷✷✷✷✷✷✷

Regions	Canton Valais, originally from Geneva, French-speaking Switzerland in general. Costume of Evolena, Valais. Plate 3.	
Character	Simple and flowing.	
Formation	Couples face C-C, men on L of women.	

Dance	MUSIC
Start each figure with outside foot.	*Bars*
	A
1 3 slow walking steps forward (one step to each bar), face partners and clap hands on third beat of 3rd bar and on first beat of 4th bar.	1–4
Repeat walks and claps three times.	5–16
	B
2 Holding inside hands, 16 Waltz steps forwards swinging the joined hands forward and backward to shoulder height.	17–32
N.B.—In Waltz step feet pass each other on second and third beats as in triple run.	
	C
3 Couples join in Closed grasp, 16 Waltz steps turning, moving round the room as in an old-time waltz.	33–40 repeated
Repeat from the beginning as often as desired.	

VALSE FRAPPÉE

Valais, Geneva etc.
Arranged by Arnold Foster

C

Play A, B, C C.

A MOLÉSON

Region	Gruyère, Canton Fribourg. Plate 4.
Character	Simple singing dance. A Coraule.
Formation	Couples hold hands in a circle, men on L of women.

Dance	MUSIC
Start each figure with l foot, except in the 2nd figure where the woman begins with r foot.	*Bars*
	A
1 10 walking steps C, closing feet together on the eleventh step to face centre of circle, and hold on the twelfth beat. Repeat C-C.	1–4 repeated
9 Gallop steps C, finishing with a step to L, and close feet together.	5–8
Clap hands and bow to contrary partner (clap on accented note marked Λ).	8–9
Clap hands and bow to own partner (clap on accented note marked Λ).	9–10
	B
2 Couples join in Waltz grasp: 16 Schottische steps turning to R and travelling C-C.	11–18 repeated
N.B.—The timing of the step is 'I and 2, 3' as described in Schottische step A.	

Plate 3
Valse Frappée. Evolena, Valais

Plate 4
A Moléson. Gruyère

A MOLÉSON

From Gruyère
Arranged by Arnold Foster

Play three times with repeats.

	A
3 Repeat 1st figure.	1–4 repeated 5–10
4 Partners join in Trüll grasp and travel C-C—i.e. men forward and women backward—16 Schottische steps, women turning under the joined r arms (two steps for one turn) while the men travel forward with no turn.	B 11 18 repeated
5 Repeat 1st figure.	A 1–10 as above
6 Repeat 2nd figure.	B 11–18 repeated

ALEWANDER—ALLEMANDE

Region   Engelberg, Obwalden. Plate 2.

Character   Simple walking dance.

Formation   Eight couples with hands joined in a circle, men on L of women.

Dance Begin each figure with 1 foot.	MUSIC *Bars*
1 *Circle* 16 walking steps C, stamping on the last step; 16 walking steps C-C, stamping on the last step.	A 1–8 1–8
2 *Women pass by* Women dance C with 32 walking steps, passing alternately in front of and behind the men. At the same time the men walk backward with 3 steps and a stamp as the women pass in front of them; they then move forward to the centre with 3 steps and a stamp as the women pass behind them. They continue backwards and forwards alternately until the women are back to place.	B 9–24
3 *Turn partners* Hands crossed behind backs, resting hands on partners' hips: 16 walking steps turning C-C on spot and stamping on the last	C 25–32 repeated

ALEWANDER

From Engelberg
Arranged by Arnold Foster

35

Play A A, B, C C, A A.   *The speed of last* A *to be* Presto.

step; 16 walking steps turning C on spot
and stamping on the last step, to finish
in a circle as at beginning.

4 *Circle Gallop*   A
    16 Gallop steps C, jumping feet together on   1–8
    the eighth step.
    16 Gallop steps C-C, jumping feet together   1–8
    on the eighth step.

LÜDEREN POLKA

Region   Emmental, Canton Berne. Plate 1.

Character   Gay.

Formation Couples face C-C, men on L of women.

Dance	MUSIC *Bars*
1 Hands on hips :—	A
One Polka step away from partner.	1
One Polka step towards partner.	2
Closed grasp :—	
4 Spring Waltz or Step Hops turning with partner.	3–4
Repeat the Polka and Waltz steps.	5–8
Repeat the whole figure.	1–8
2 Waist grasp :—	B
One Rheinländer step on 1 foot, moving diagonally forward to L.	9
One Rheinländer step on r foot, moving diagonally forward to R.	10
4 Step Hops turning to L about, man dancing on the spot and swinging his partner round.	11–12
Repeat Rheinländer and turning steps.	13–16
Repeat the whole figure.	9–16

LÜDEREN POLKA

From the Emmental
Arranged by Arnold Foster

Play A A, B B, C, A A.

3 Arch grasp:—	C
One Rheinländer step on l foot.	17
One Rheinländer step on r foot.	18
The man stands still and turns the woman a quarter-turn in front of him to L, the woman bending her knees slightly and looking at her partner over her l shoulder; the man then twists the woman a half-turn to R, so that she looks at him over her r shoulder with another small curtsey. (Half a bar to each turn.)	19
The woman turns to L about under her own r arm with 4 quick walks on spot.	20
Repeat the movements of bars 17–20 twice.	21–28
4 Hands on hips:—	A
Repeat the 1st figure.	1–8 repeated

BIBLIOGRAPHY

BORDIER, PIERRE.—*Dances Populaires Suisses.* 4th series. Geneva.

BROCKMANN-JEROSCH, H.—*La Terre Helvétique.* Version française. Neuchâtel, 1930–31.

MOSER-GOSSWEILER, F.—*Volksbräuche der Schweiz.* Zurich, 1940. (These two for folklore and pictures of Carnival dancers.)

WITZIG, LOUISE, and STERN, ALFRED.—*Volkstänze der Schweiz.* Vol. 1, 2nd ed. Zurich.

WITZIG, LOUISE, and STERN, ALFRED.—*12 Schweizer Tänze.* 3rd ed. Hug & Co., Zurich.

WITZIG, LOUISE, and STERN, ALFRED.—*Schweizer Tänze.* Blattausgabe, 7–12. (Edition in separate sheets. Nos. 1–6 to be found in *12 Schweizer Tänze,* above.)

MUSIC

AESCHBACHER, KARL.—*Appenzeller Volkstänze.* 2 vols. Appenzell a.Rh.

GASSMANN, A. L.—*D' Ländlermusik: 100 Ländler und Buuretänz für Solo-Klarinette und Trompete mit Begleitung der Handorgel und des Kontrabasses.* Zurich.

STERN, ALFRED.—*12 Tanzweisen für Klavier oder 2 Geigen und Cello.* Hug & Co., Zurich. (Tunes for *Volkstänze der Schweiz,* see above.)